Railway
Trivia

COMPILED BY
Alan M. Drewett

For my Father
William George Drewett
1922–1987
with love and gratitude

First published by Alan M. Drewett 1989.

Copyright Alan M. Drewett 1989.

Printed and bound by Stoate & Bishop (Printers) Ltd.

ISBN 0 9514591 0 4

Introduction

If you have ever been bored by railways then this is probably the book that you have been waiting for. You know the sort of times: waiting on an otherwise lifeless station for a late running connection; staring at the darkness through the window of a late running connection or just being frustrated by your inability to understand life's more interesting people, clad as they often are in anoraks with notebooks stuffed in the pockets.

If so, then help is at hand. Herein are 720 gems of information about Britain's railways, mainly from the time of World War One until the late 1980s. Each one has been carefully chosen for its enlightenment and entertainment value from literally dozens of railway guides and textbooks and so saves you the bother of reading them all yourself. They have been arranged in the following six categories:

L Locomotives and rolling stock.
C Civil Engineering and track.
S Stations and notable train services.
R Railway Companies, building and operating.
T Technology on the railways.
P Personalities, affecting, or affected by, railways.

This makes them compatible with other trivia-type games and books as well as suitable for the following pastimes:

Trivia Solitaire

Look at each facing page in turn. Write down your answers to the questions then turn the page to see how many were correct. Repeat this until you can remember all 720 facts.

Trivia Challenge

In a group, elect a quizmaster to hold the book and keep score. In any order agreed, the quizmaster asks each player to choose a letter and answer the relevant question in the first block. If he is correct, the player selects a different letter in the next block and continues. If he is incorrect, the question is handed to the next player in turn. If no-one knows the answer the quizmaster may reveal it and pick another question in the same or next block for the first player. Each correct answer scores one point.

Frontispiece: A 'Peak' diesel-electric locomotive arrives at Gloucester Eastgate station with a train from the North. From this early 1960s view only the Horton Road gasometer survives. A host of fine detail has been lost forever in terms of locomotives, rolling stock, track, station buildings and technical installations. What is commonplace today is rare tomorrow and gone the day after that. 'Twas ever thus.

Photo by W.G. Drewett

Q1   **L** How many Eastenders will this train take home? *(A.M. Drewett)*

Q1   **L** How many able bodied people can a Docklands Light Railway train seat?
      C In which year was the Severn Tunnel opened?
      S Between which two cities does the 'Mayflower' express train run?
      R D2999, 'Falcon' and 'Kestrel' were all prototypes from which manufacturing company?
      T What transmission feature is common to 'Black Fives' 44738-57 and 71000 'Duke of Gloucester'?
      P In 1988 who was Director of British Rail's Inter-City sector?

Q2   **L** Who manufactured the engines for 'Warship' D830 'Majestic'?
      C Where is the World's first iron railway bridge now on show?
      S In which month and year were train services withdrawn from Bampton, Devon?
      R For which railroads centenary did 4-6-0 'King George V' travel to the U.S.A.?
      T Which type of power plant did a.c. electric E2001 have in 1956?
      P Who designed the L.N.E.R. Class J94 0-6-0- ST engines?

Q3   **L** What type of vehicle is a Great Western 'Toad'?
      C Which is the longest railway bridge in Britain?
      S Between which two stations in East Anglia did 'The Rhinelander' service run?
      R How many 'Pacific' type locomotives did the G.W.R. ever build?
      T For what purpose is a Pandrol Clip used?
      P Who played 'Buster' in the film about the Great Train Robbery?

A1   **L** 84.
      C 1886.
      S London and Plymouth.
      R Brush Traction Limited.
      T Caprotti valve gear.
      P Dr. John Prideaux.

A2   **L** Davey Paxman.
      C The National Railway Museum, York.
      S October 1963.
      R The Baltimore and Ohio Railroad.
      T Gas turbine. (It was then numbered 18100.)
      P Robert A. Riddles C.B.E.

A3   **L** A brake van.
      C The Tay Bridge.
      S Harwich Parkeston Quay and Stowmarket.
      R One.
      T Holding rails to their sleepers.
      P Phil Collins.

Q5   **L** What made this locomotive famous in July 1938? *(A.O. Wynn)*

Q4
  L Which 'Britannia' pacific was displayed at the Festival of Britain?
  C Which British railway bridge has the two longest spans?
  S Which named Inverness-Kyle of Lochalsh service has an observation car?
  R How was the B.R. crest depicted on D1000?
  T 56 feet 11 inches and 63 feet 5 inches are standard lengths of what?
  P Who was Chairman of British Rail in 1988?

Q5
  L Which Gresley Pacific holds the World steam speed record?
  C Which is Britain's tallest viaduct?
  S What is the name of the station between Lancaster and Morecambe?
  R Which company supplied the British Rail class 91 engine?
  T From what material are the rails of Forest Railroad Park, Cornwall made?
  P In which Norman Wisdom film did a Blue Pullman D.M.U. appear?

Q6
  L Which is the oldest of the three 'Vale of Rheidol' engines?
  C In 1980, where was the longest length of straight B.R. track located?
  S Where does 'The Essex Continental' run to from London?
  R When did the Midland Railway build Britains only 0-10-0 tender engine?
  T Who built the 'Co-Bo' diesels of British Rail?
  P Who closed the last rivet of the Forth Bridge on 4 March 1890?

Q7
  L To which class does the L.M.S. engine 'Kolhapur' belong?
  C How many feet above sea level is Druimuachdar Summit?
  S What is the southern terminus of 'The Wessex Scot' service?
  R In D.M.U. parlance, what do the initials B.U.T. stand for?
  T In the absence of welding, how are adjoining rail sections held together?
  P Which ex-Radio One D.J. said 'This is the age of the train'?

Q8
  L Which locomotive killed Mr. William Huskisson M.P. in 1830?
  C How long is Blea Moor Tunnel between Settle Junction and Carlisle?
  S Which London station is terminus of 'The Night Aberdonian'?
  R How many locomotives did B.R. inherit on 1 January 1948?
  T What do the initials M.A.S. stand for?
  P Which 'St. Trinians' film featured a train chase sequence?

A4
L 70004 'William Shakespeare'.
C The Forth Bridge.
S 'The Hebridean'.
R As a polished aluminium bas-relief.
T British Rail Diesel Multiple Unit underframes.
P Sir Robert Reid.

A5
L 4468 'Mallard'.
C Ballochmyle Viaduct, Scotland.
S Bare Lane.
R G.E.C.
T Aluminium alloy.
P 'The Early Bird'.

A6
L 9 'Prince of Wales'.
C Between Selby and Hull.
S Harwich Town.
R 1920.
T Metropolitan Vickers.
P The Prince of Wales (later Edward VII).

A7
L 'Jubilee'.
C 1484 feet.
S Poole, Dorset.
R British United Traction.
T By means of fishplates.
P Jimmy Savile O.B.E.

A8
L George Stephenson's 'Rocket'.
C 1 mile 869 yards.
S Kings Cross.
R 20445.
T Multiple Aspect Signalling.
P 'The Great St. Trinians Train Robbery'.

Q9   **L**   'Castle' 5063 'Earl Baldwin' hurries through Gloucester Central.

(W.G. Drewett)

Q9   **L**   Which G.W.R. 'Castle' is preserved at the Science Museum, London?
     C   How many operational B.R. tunnels are over 3 miles long?
     S   Where do the lines from Pwllheli and Aberystwyth meet?
     R   In 1959, how many types of 0-4-0 and 0-6-0 diesel were in B.R. service?
     T   Why were B.R. '9F's 92165-92167 easy to fire?
     P   Who did 34010 'Sidmouth' bring to Waterloo on a state visit in 1959?

Q10 **L**   What number did G.W.R. locomotive 'City of Truro' carry in 1904?
     C   In 1980, how many S.R. lines were cleared for 100 m.p.h. working?
     S   What was unusual about the former Barton Gates signal box, Gloucester?
     R   Wilkes and Ashmore styled which Brush Type 2 class?
     T   Which maximum boiler pressure had the Hawksworth 'Counties' in 1945?
     P   What did William Milner win at York Station on 29 April 1942?

Q11 **L**   What are B.R. Class 35 diesel locomotives also known as?
     C   How many feet above sea level is Shap Summit?
     S   Which is Britain's most northerly railway station?
     R   Which railway introduced Britain's only 2-8-2T design in 1934?
     T   What aids to steam traction were found in the Standedge Tunnels?
     P   Who starred in 'The Thirty Nine Steps', shot on the S.V.R.?

Q16 **T** Thoroughly modern track (see also **Q83-T**) *(A.M. Drewett)*.

A9 **L** 4073 'Caerphilly Castle'.
  C Three.
  S Dovey Junction.
  R Twenty.
  T They had mechanical stokers.
  P The Shah of Iran.

A10 **L** 3440
  C None.
  S It was mounted on a gantry over the tracks.
  R Class 31.
  T 280 pounds per square inch.
  P The King's Commendation for Gallantry.

A11 **L** 'Hymeks'.
  C 915 feet.
  S Thurso, Scotland.
  R The Great Western Railway.
  T Water troughs.
  P Robert Powell.

Q12
L S.R. class 'V' engines were all named after what?
C Which of the South Devon inclines is located between Newton Abbot and Totnes?
S Which Cornish landmark featured on the windows of the Penzance–Aberdeen 'Cornishman'?
R How many '4F' 0-6-0 engines were built by the M.R. and L.M.S.R.?
T Which sub-division of B.R. Class 33 has buckeye couplings?
P Who had a hit record with 'Waterloo Sunset'?

Q13
L Which Liverpool and Manchester engine featured in an Ealing film?
C West of Paddington, where does the speed limit first rise above 100 m.p.h.?
S From which city did 'The Master Cutler' Pullman run to London?
R In which city is the National Railway Museum located?
T What fuel did S.R. 'T9' No. 121 burn experimentally during 1947?
P Which railway had J.G. Robinson as C.M.E. from 1900 to 1922?

Q14
L How many v-shaped 'whiskers' does the prototype 'Deltic' have at each nose end?
C How long is Barmouth Estuary Bridge?
S In July 1960, where did 'The Kings Cross Freighter' run from London?
R What was the Manchester, Sheffield and Lincoln Railway later known as?
T Which Italian invention was built into ten B.R. '9F's in 1955?
P Which now-preserved line featured in the Beatles 'A Hard Day's Night'?

Q15
L In which year did the L.M.S.R. introduce its 'Princess Coronation' class?
C In 1980, where was Britain's most northerly hump marshalling yard?
S Where does 'The Orcadian' service run to from Thurso and Wick?
R Which one of the 'Big Four' did not use water troughs for its steam engines?
T What type of rail requires a 'key' to hold it to a 'chair'?
P Who lives at 'Silver Cedars, High Bannerdown, Batheaston, Bath'?

Q16
L Which B.R. '9F' was not outshopped in black unlined livery?
C What was the Britannia Tubular Bridge built to span?
S Which service had a St. Christopher medal on its window stickers?
R Which railway operated trains between Evercreech Junction and Bath?
T What type of rail is improved in durability by a 'sole plate'?
P Which S.R. locomotive designer had the names Oliver Vaughan Snell?

A12 L Public Schools.
     C Dainton Incline.
     S St. Michaels Mount.
     R 772.
     T Class 33/1.
     P The Kinks.

A13 L 'Lion'.
     C Acton.
     S Sheffield.
     R York.
     T Oil.
     P The Great Central Railway.

A14 L Three.
     C 2500 feet.
     S Newcastle-upon-Tyne.
     R The Great Central Railway.
     T The Crosti boiler.
     P The West Somerset Railway.

A15 L 1937.
     C Millerhill, Glasgow.
     S Inverness.
     R The Southern Railway.
     T Bull-head section rail.
     P O.S. Nock.

A16 L 92220 'Evening Star'.
     C The Menai Straits between North Wales and Anglesea.
     S 'The Talisman'.
     R The Somerset and Dorset Joint Railway.
     T Flat bottomed rail.
     P Bulleid.

Q18   **C** 'Hymek' D7024 arrives at Kemble during August 1963 *(W.G. Drewett)*.

Q17   **L**   Class E.M.1 electric engine 26000 was known as what?
         C   Of what material is Glenfinnan Viaduct, Scotland, made?
         S   Which is Britain's most northerly railway junction?
         R   Which railway painted its locomotives 'haematite' red?
         T   What transmission system did Gas Turbine locomotive G.T.3 use?
         P   Who led the violent robbery of service IM44 on 8 August 1963?

Q18   **L**   The Yorkshire Engine Co. 0-8-0 D/H design of 1961 was called what?
         C   How many running lines link Swindon and Kemble, Gloucestershire?
         S   What other word do the station names of Didcot, Tiverton and Bodmin contain?
         R   Which railway adorned its stock with 'Sunshine' lettering?
         T   On the G.W.R., how were rail-holding chairs usually fixed to the sleepers?
         P   Who vied with Sir Humphrey Davey to invent a miner's safety lamp?

Q19   **L**   What were B.R. standard pacifics 72000–72009 named after?
         C   Which river does Brunel's Royal Albert Bridge span?
         S   What is the Cardiff-Holyhead 'Y Cymru' service called in English?
         R   Which railway had the motto 'Dominic Dirige Nos Vertute et Industria'?
         T   In Whyte notation, what is a 2-6-0 engine called?
         P   In 1987, which railway magazine had Roger Wood as its editor?

A17 **L** 'Tommy'.
  C Concrete.
  S Georgemas Junction, where the Thurso and Wick lines diverge.
  R The Furness Railway.
  T Mechanical.
  P Ronald Biggs.

A18 **L** 'Taurus'.
  C One.
  S 'Parkway'.
  R The Southern Railway.
  T By means of bolts (other lines used spikes).
  P George Stephenson.

A19 **L** Scottish Clans.
  C The River Tamar.
  S 'The Welshman'.
  R The Great Western Railway.
  T Mogul.
  P 'Motive Power Monthly'.

Q23 **C** This little engine made it to the top! *(W.G. Drewett)*

Q20
L Which d.c. electric class was named after Greek Mythological figures?
C What material was the original Ponsanooth Viaduct, Cornwall, mainly built of?
S Which city has stations named Westgate and Kirkgate?
R In which year was the current Inter-City 'Executive' livery introduced?
T How many piston strokes per cycle are there in a 'Deltic' diesel engine?
P What was Isambard Brunel's mother's maiden name?

Q21
L What were the first 35 examples of L.N.E.R. Class B1 named after?
C Which railway tubular bridge was designed with optional chain suspension by Robert Stephenson?
S Which animal appeared on the window stickers of 'The Principality' service?
R Which railway first painted its locomotives in 'Crimson Lake'?
T Which two British softwoods were most popular for sleeper making?
P In 1987 which B.R. sector had Chris Green as its director?

Q22
L Which name has L.N.E.R. 'V2' 60847 passed on to H.S.T. power car 43152?
C Between which two stations is 'Brunel's Billiard Table' to be found?
S Which city used to have a station named Green Park?
R What do the initials B.R.E.L. stand for?
T Which 'Big Four' company uniquely used lower quadrant signals?
P From which organisation did Dr Richard Beeching move to B.R.?

Q23
L How many driving wheels does D200 have?
C Which section of the Cambrian Railway contained its steepest incline?
S Which E.C.M.L. service featured three castles on its window stickers?
R Where were the locomotive works of the L. and Y.R. located?
T B.R. Standard '2' Prarie tanks were all fitted for what?
P What government office was held by David Mitchell M.P. in 1987?

Q24
L Where is G.W.R. pannier tank 9400 preserved?
C Between which two stations is Sapperton tunnel located?
S Which station re-opened on 2 October 1987?
R Which railway had 'Plum and Spilt Milk' as its coach livery?
T What method of train description do D5500 and D8000 share?
P Who was the first private citizen to own A3 pacific 'Flying Scotsman'?

A20 **L** E.M.2.
   C Wood.
   S Wakefield.
   R 1983.
   T Two.
   P Sophia Kingdom.

A21 **L** African antelopes.
   C The Britannia Bridge, across the Menai Straits.
   S The Welsh Dragon.
   R The Midland Railway.
   T Pine and Douglas Fir.
   P Network South East.

A22 **L** 'St. Peters School York A.D. 627'.
   C London Paddington and Swindon.
   S Bath.
   R British Rail Engineering Limited.
   T The Great Western Railway.
   P I.C.I.

A23 **L** Twelve.
   C The Welshpool and Llanfair Railway.
   S 'The Newcastle Executive'.
   R Horwich.
   T Push-pull working.
   P Minister of State for Transport.

A24 **L** Swindon Railway Museum.
   C Stroud and Kemble.
   S Birmingham Snow Hill.
   R The Caledonian Railway.
   T Discs.
   P Alan Pegler.

Q25 **S** What is the building in question? *(A.M. Drewett)*

Q25 **L** What were S.R. 'N15' and B.R. Standard '5' locomotives named after?
  C In which year did the Severn Railway Bridge open?
  S Which building featured on the window stickers of the 'Cheltenham Spa Express'?
  R Which B.R. sector has a swift as its symbol?
  T In British track laying, how many wooden sleepers supported each 60 feet of rails?
  P Who officially opened the Docklands Light Railway on 30 July 1987?

Q26 **L** How many B.R. Class 47/4 diesels are named after universities?
  C Which railway is crossed by Paper Mill and Hood Bridges?
  S What feature links the stations at Tamworth and Shotton, Clwyd?
  R What do the initials C.I.E. stand for?
  T Which B.R. coaching sub-mark introduced fluorescent light in compartments?
  P What did Patrick Stirling liken to 'a laddie running wi' his breeks doon'?

Q27 **L** Which G.W.R. 'Dukedog' name is carried on by diesel 37671?
  C Where did most of the stone used in building Swindon Works come from?
  S What is the eastern terminus of 'The East Anglian' service?
  R Which railway had its works at St. Rollox, Glasgow?
  T Why could G.W.R. engines 6700–6779 not haul passenger trains?
  P Michael Harris edited which railway magazine from 1977 to 1987?

Q29   **L**   Who was this before the Knighthood and a respray? *(A.M. Drewett)*

A25   **L**   Legendary Arthurian Characters.
         C   1879.
         S   Pittville Pump Room, Cheltenham.
         R   Inter-City.
         T   24.
         P   Her Majesty the Queen.

A26   **L**   Six.
         C   The Dart Valley Railway (Buckfastleigh section).
         S   Both serve two lines which cross at different levels.
         R   Coras Iompair Eireann (Irish State Railways).
         T   Mark 2a.
         P   A coupled steam locomotive.

A27   **L**   'Tre Pol and Pen'.
         C   Box Tunnel.
         S   Norwich.
         R   The Caledonian Railway.
         T   They lacked vacuum brakes.
         P   'Railway World'.

Q28
- **L** Electroputere of Romania built the first 30 members of which B.R. class?
- **C** In which year did both Forth bridges appear on a 3d British stamp?
- **S** Which city has B.R. stations named Victoria and Piccadilly?
- **R** First class N.E.R. coaches had what colour upholstery?
- **T** Thornton Yard, Fife, was the first in Britain to be monitored by what?
- **P** Who was the last C.M.E. of the London and South Western Railway?

Q29
- **L** What was diesel 50007 'Sir Edward Elgar' originally named?
- **C** How many viaducts separate Paignton and Kingswear Stations?
- **S** Which 'Big Four' company introduced 'The Bristolian' service?
- **R** Blue and yellow wavy lines feature in which Railfreight sub-sector symbol?
- **T** How long is a standard British wooden sleeper?
- **P** Which light railway builder founded the K. and E.S.R.?

Q30
- **L** In December 1986, which B.R. class had 4 members named after power stations?
- **C** In which year did the G.W.R. begin making its own rails at Swindon?
- **S** Which town has stations named Forster Square and Interchange?
- **R** Which 3 owners have both the Vale of Rheidol and W. and L. Railways shared?
- **T** 'Spanner Swirlyflo' and 'Clarkson' are both makes of what?
- **P** Who was popularly known as 'Concrete Bob'?

Q31
- **L** Which Class 59 diesel carries a bell on the front of its Number 1 end cab?
- **C** How did Moseley Green Tunnel, Gloucestershire, help the 1939–1945 war effort?
- **S** 'The Hook Continental' and 'The European' meet the ferries where?
- **R** Until 1 October 1936, who operated the Midland and G.N. Joint Line?
- **T** What would a Pratt-Truss gantry be used to support?
- **P** Who preceded Sir Robert Reid as Chairman of British Rail?

Q32
- **L** How many second class seats are there in a Trailer Guard Second?
- **C** Which G.W.R. subsidiary was narrowed to 4'8½" in May 1872?
- **S** Which town has stations named Warrior Square and West Street?
- **R** Until 1923, how many independent railways served the Isle of Wight?
- **T** Where in a steam locomotive is a snifting valve found?
- **P** Which station bears a memorial to Miss Emma Saunders?

A28 **L** Class 56.
      C 1964.
      S Manchester.
      R Dark blue.
      T Closed circuit television.
      P R.W. Urie.

A29 **L** 'Hercules'.
      C Four.
      S The Great Western Railway.
      R Railfreight Petroleum.
      T 8 feet 6 inches.
      P Colonel Holman F. Stephens.

A30 **L** Class 58.
      C 1861.
      S Bradford, West Yorkshire.
      R The Cambrian Railway, The G.W.R. and British Railways.
      T Train heating boiler.
      P Sir Robert McAlpine.

A31 **L** 59001 'Yeoman Endeavour'.
      C As an ammunition dump.
      S Harwich Parkeston Quay.
      R The L.M.S.R. and L.N.E.R.
      T Semaphore signals.
      P Sir Peter Parker.

A32 **L** 63.
      C The South Wales Railway.
      S St. Leonards, Sussex.
      R Three.
      T In the smokebox.
      P Bristol Temple Meads.

Q34 **T** Signal cabin and starting signal at Cromer, Norfolk. *(A.M. Drewett).*

Q33 **L** '4F' 0-6-0 44026 was the last M.R. engine to be built before what?
C In which month and year was the Severn Bridge breached by barges?
S Where does 'The Fenman' service run from London Liverpool Street?
R In which year was the Weston, Clevedon and Portishead Railway absorbed by the G.W.R.?
T What keeps the brakes 'off' in the Westinghouse brake system?
P Vic Berry and Dai Woodham are famous for turning locomotives into what?

Q34 **L** What was 46202 'Princess Anne' known as when built by the L.M.S.R.?
C Who designed Kilsby Tunnel and the Britannia Tubular Bridge?
S New Street and Moor Street Stations are found in which city?
R Which county was home to the Leek and Manifold Light Railway?
T What does a diamond shaped white plate on a signal post indicate?
P Who played the female 'Railway Children' in the 1970's film of the book?

Q35 **L** What name was given to Bulleid 'Tavern' buffet car S7897?
C How many times does the Whitby-Grosmont line cross the River Esk?
S Which city has stations named Temple Meads and Parkway?
R During the 1930s, which of the 'Big Four' had the smallest fleet of streamlined engines?
T Where in a steam locomotive is a brick arch to be found?
P Which preserved railway was founded by artist David Shepherd?

A33 **L** Grouping, in 1923.
        C October 1960.
        S Kings Lynn.
        R 1940.
        T Positive air pressure above atmospheric level.
        P Scrap metal.

A34 **L** 'Turbomotive'.
        C Robert Stephenson.
        S Birmingham.
        R Staffordshire.
        T That track circuiting is in use.
        P Jenny Agutter and Sally Thomsett.

A35 **L** 'At the Sign of the Three Plovers'.
        C Nine.
        S Bristol.
        R The Great Western Railway.
        T The firebox.
        P The East Somerset Railway.

A36 P
Statue of Isambard Kingdom Brunel at Paddington *(A.M. Drewett)*

Q36
L Which G.W.R. vehicle is most associated with Palethorpes sausage traffic?
C For what railway purpose is stone from Whitecliffe Quarry, Coleford, used?
S Where does 'The Humber-Lincs Executive' run to from London?
R In which year was the brand name 'Inter-City' first applied to B.R. services?
T In four aspect signalling, what follows single amber?
P In which town was Isambard Kingdom Brunel born in 1806?

Q37
L What was the English Electric gas turbine 4-6-0 of 1961 known as?
C Swithland Viaduct carries the Great Central Railway over what?
S Where does 'The West Yorkshire Executive' run from London?
R When was the Hull and Barnsley Railway taken over by the N.E.R.?
T How is the energy of an electric engine dissipated in rheostatic braking?
P Which ex-Beatle narrates the T.V. Series 'Thomas the Tank Engine'?

Q38
L 'Leicestershire and Derbyshire Yeomanry' was the only 'namer' of which B.R. class?
C Which organisation levelled Norchard Steam Centres site in 1974?
S Which station has the longest platform in Britain?
R How many Metropolitan locomotives transferred to the L.N.E.R. in November 1937?
T What voltage flows through the overhead wires of the W.C.M.L.?
P H.F.S. Morgan, the sports car maker, was once a draughtsman for who?

Q39
L How many Bulleid 'Leader' class engines were ever steamed?
C Which station marked the summit of the Lynton and Barnstaple Railway?
S How far north does 'The Highland Chieftain' H.S.T. service travel?
R Which one of the 'Big Four' did the Knott End Railway join in 1923?
T In Whyte notation, what is a 2-8-0 wheel arrangement called?
P Sir Vincent L. Raven was the last C.M.E. of which railway?

Q40
L Which G.W.R. mixed traffic engines had straight name plates?
C What is the maximum headroom on the Burry Port and Gwendraeth Valley line?
S Who designed the terminal station at Bristol Temple Meads?
R The L.T. steam locomotives had which colours of lining out?
T What does a mercury arc rectifier do in d.c. electric traction?
P In 1987, Bob Bayman was operations manager of which railway?

A36
  L Siphon 'G'.
  C Ballast for high speed train lines.
  S Grimsby Town.
  R 1966.
  T Double amber.
  P Portsmouth.

A37
  L G.T.3.
  C Swithland Reservoir.
  S Leeds.
  R 1922.
  T By means of heat.
  P Ringo Starr.

A38
  L Class 46.
  C The Army Apprentices College, Beachley.
  S Gloucester.
  R 18.
  T 25000 volts.
  P The Great Western Railway, at Swindon Works.

A39
  L One.
  C Woody Bay.
  S Inverness.
  R The London, Midland and Scottish Railway.
  T 'Consolidation'.
  P The North Eastern Railway.

A40
  L The Hawksworth 'Counties'.
  C 11 feet 10 inches.
  S Isambard Kingdom Brunel.
  R Black and yellow.
  T Reducing voltage and converting alternating to direct current.
  P The Docklands Light Railway.

Q43　**R** 7819 'Hinton Manor' waits at Bridgnorth. *(A.M. Drewett)*

Q41　**L** What first travelled to Ramsgate on 3 June 1959?
　　　C For whom was the Shakespeare's Cliff Tunnel, near Dover, built?
　　　S Which is the London terminus of 'The Bradford Executive'?
　　　R The two-tone livery of B.R. Classes 47 and 55 contained which shades of green?
　　　T Which part of Bulleids 'Merchant Navy' pacifics featured a thermic syphon?
　　　P John A. Coiley is keeper of which museum?

Q42　**L** The first Derby-built diesel-electric under the 1955 Modernisation plan had what number?
　　　C Who designed Watford Tunnel for the London and Birmingham Railway?
　　　S Which town used to have stations named Malvern Road and St. James?
　　　R Which railway was incorporated by Act of Parliament on 31 August 1835?
　　　T What device collects current from overhead wires?
　　　P Which railway knight was christened 'Herbert Nigel'?

Q43　**L** The last pre-Nationalisation design steam engine was built where?
　　　C Where is the winding engine of Weatherhill Incline preserved?
　　　S How far north does 'The Cleveland Executive' service travel?
　　　R Which preserved railway links Bridgnorth with Kidderminster?
　　　T Which type of Semaphore signal has a notch cut in its end?
　　　P Who was C.M.E. of the G.W.R. from 1921 to 1941?

Q45 **L** 03061, 25116 in blue and a maroon 'Western'. Swindon 1980.

(A.M. Drewett)

A41 **L** An Electric Multiple Unit.
      C The South Eastern and Chatham Railway.
      S Kings Cross.
      R Brunswick (upper) and Apple (lower).
      T The firebox.
      P The National Railway Museum, York.

A42 **L** D5000 (later Class 24).
      C Robert Stephenson.
      S Cheltenham Spa.
      R The Great Western Railway.
      T A pantograph.
      P Sir H.N. Gresley.

A43 **L** Swindon Works.
      C The National Railway Museum, York.
      S Sunderland.
      R The Severn Valley Railway.
      T Distant signal.
      P Charles B. Collett.

Q44
L A4 Pacific 4469 and G.W.R. 4911 'Bowden Hall' were destroyed by what?
C Sir Thomas Bouch designed the first bridge over which Scottish Firth?
S Which city has stations named St. Davids and St. Thomas?
R The cab window sills of B.R. Classes 26, 35 and 55 were what colour when new?
T What voltage was used in the Manchester-Sheffield-Wath electrification?
P What relation are writers Cecil J. and Geoffery Freeman Allen?

Q45
L In what colour was D1000 'Western Enterprise' outshopped in 1961?
C Which company originally owned Willington Dene Viaduct?
S To which city does 'The Night Scotsman' sleeper service run?
R Which railway promoted itself as 'The Premier Line'?
T Which engine was first to be evaluated at the Rugby Test Plant in 1948?
P What concept did Henry Booth of Liverpool suggest to George Stephenson?

Q46
L How many Class 08 shunters became Class 13 units in 1965?
C The girder bridge south of York station celebrates which Archbishop?
S Where does 'The Yorkshire Pullman' run from London Kings Cross?
R In which year did the Talyllyn become a preserved railway?
T Which of the 'Big Four' had the largest network of three-rail electrified lines?
P Who served as C.M.E. of the G.W.R. from 1916 to 1921?

Q47
L When was the last second-class side corridor coach built for B.R.?
C Which Welsh railway features a spiral of track to gain height?
S Which city has stations named Queen Street and St. Enochs?
R Which railway company has its locomotive works at Boston Lodge?
T What feature has a Siphon 'G' milk van to allow churns to cool quickly?
P Who presented 'Confessions of a Trainspotter' for B.B.C. television in 1980?

Q48
L What was the number of B.R.s first pilot scheme diesel, delivered in 1957?
C Until 1935, which section of the S.R. contained its highest point?
S Which U.K. city has stations named Central and York Road?
R Which was the first London depot to handle High Speed Trains?
T What type of control system is fitted to Class 86 electric engines?
P Who was Honorary President of the International Railway Congress in 1954?

A44   **L** The Luftwaffe.
         C The Firth of Tay.
         S Exeter.
         R White.
         T 1500 volts d.c.
         P Father and son.

A45   **L** Desert Sand.
         C The Newcastle, North Shields and Tyne Railway.
         S Edinburgh.
         R The London and North Western Railway.
         T 60007 'Sir Nigel Gresley'.
         P The multi-tubular boiler.

A46   **L** Six.
         C Archbishop Holgate.
         S Leeds.
         R 1951.
         T The Southern Railway.
         P George Jackson Churchward.

A47   **L** 1962.
         C The Ffestiniog Railway.
         S Glasgow.
         R The Ffestiniog Railway.
         T Concrete floors.
         P Michael Palin.

A48   **L** D8000.
         C The Lynton and Barnstaple Railway.
         S Belfast.
         R Old Oak Common, Western Region.
         T High tension tap changing.
         P The Duke of Gloucester.

Q49 C Where will the real road traffic go in 1993? *(A.M. Drewett)*

Q49 **L** What name linked G.W.R. engine 6028 and L.M.S. 6244?
     C Which motorway will serve the British terminal of the Channel Tunnel?
     S Which is the London terminus for the Manchester Pullman services?
     R Which railway ran its first public train on 27 September 1825?
     T What feature did Talyllyn Railway engine 'Edward Thomas' share with '9F' 92250?
     P Who starred in 'Yanks', shot mainly on the Worth Valley Railway?

Q50 **L** On which railway do Double Fairlie engines run in Wales?
     C In which year was Box Tunnel of the G.W.R. opened?
     S Which named express links Hereford and Worcester with London?
     R How many lions support the crest of the British Pullman company?
     T How many rails are needed in the L.T. electrification system?
     P Ffestiniog Railway engine 'Earl of Merioneth' is named after which Royal person?

Q51 **L** B.R.1.G., B.R.3 and B.R.2.A. are types of what vehicle?
     C What type of vehicle was the Hay Inclined Plane, Shropshire, built to carry?
     S Where does the electric-hauled Royal Scot Limited run to?
     R Which one of the 'Big Four' had chocolate and cream coaches?
     T A Hallade recorder is mounted on a train to assess the state of what?
     P Which British Prime Minister saw the L. and M.R. open in 1830?

A49   **L** 'King George VI'.
         C The M20.
         S Euston.
         R The Stockton and Darlington Railway.
         T A Giesel ejector.
         P Richard Gere.

A50   **L** The Ffestiniog Railway.
         C 1841.
         S 'The Cathedrals Express'.
         R Two.
         T Four.
         P H.R.H. Prince Phillip.

A51   **L** Steam locomotive tenders.
         C Canal boats.
         S Glasgow.
         R The Great Western Railway.
         T Track.
         P The Duke of Wellington.

A55   **L** 08621 rests at Gloucester early in 1988. *(A.M. Drewett)*

Q52
L 'Rocket' and 'Novelty' competed on which railway in 1829?
C Who engineered Bangor Tunnel for the Chester and Holyhead Railway?
S The statue of George Stephenson, formerly at Euston, is now where?
R Which narrow-gauge railway closed on 29 September 1935?
T What voltage is used on the three-rail electrification of N.S.E.?
P Mr. A.S. Quartermaine unveiled what on Paddington Station on 29 May 1954?

Q53
L What were the L.M.S. 2-6-0 engines introduced in 1926 known as?
C Between which two stations is Morley Tunnel, E.R., located?
S Which town is served by Shaw Street Station?
R In which city would British Rail's Litchurch Lane works be found?
T What type of control system is fitted to electric engine 87101?
P Mike Smith presented which B.B.C. railway programme in 1989?

Q54
L Where is G.W.R. 4-6-0 'Lode-Star' preserved?
C Which bridge features in John Dobbin's painting of the opening of the Stockton and Darlington?
S Which London terminus was once famous for its Doric Portico?
R What was the motto of the London and North Eastern Railway?
T 'Voith' and 'Mekydro' are both types of which transmission system?
P Which publishing knight promoted the Lynton and Barnstaple Railway?

Q55
L How many traction motors has a Class 08 diesel shunter?
C What happened to the original Tay Bridge on 28 December 1879?
S Where does the 'Saint David' express run from London?
R What gauge do the Ravenglass and Eskdale and Romney, Hythe and Dymchurch Railways share?
T The stripe on the red face of a 'stop' signal arm is what colour?
P In 1980, Ralph Bennett was Chairman of which transport organisation?

Q56
L How many 'King' class engines were built by the G.W.R.?
C What happens to Box Tunnel on Isambard Brunel's birthday?
S Which railway shares Bleanau Ffestiniog station with B.R.?
R Which of the 'Big Four' published the book 'Ten Thirty Limited'?
T Why was L.M.S. engine 6202 fitted with a small second turbine?
P Which C.M.E. of the S.R. was once works manager of Inchicore, Dublin?

A52 **L** The Liverpool and Manchester Railway.
      C Robert Stephenson.
      S The National Railway Museum, York.
      R The Lynton and Barnstaple Railway.
      T 750 volts d.c.
      P A plaque to commemorate the centenary of the station.

A53 **L** 'Crabs'.
      C Batley and Morley.
      S St. Helens, Lancashire.
      R Derby.
      T Thyristor.
      P 'Railwatch'.

A54 **L** Swindon Railway Museum.
      C Skerne Bridge.
      S Euston.
      R 'Forward'.
      T Hydraulic.
      P Sir George Newnes.

A55 **L** Two.
      C It collapsed in a storm.
      S Swansea.
      R 1 foot 3 inches.
      T White.
      P London Transport.

A56 **L** Thirty.
      C The sun rises through it.
      S The Ffestiniog Railway.
      R The Great Western Railway.
      T To allow the engine to run backwards.
      P R.E.L. Maunsell.

Q57 L
When did Brush stop making these? *(A.M. Drewett)*

Q57
L When did the manufacture of B.R. Class 47 diesels cease?
C Morley Tunnel, under the Pennines, has an elliptical western portal. Who built it?
S Which of the 'Big Four' operated Wolverhampton Low Level station?
R When did B.R. abandon 'D' and 'E' prefixes on Diesel and Electric engines?
T Where was the 'B4' type coach bogie designed?
P Who designed the 'Rocket 150' stamps issued by the Royal Mail in 1980?

Q58
L When were the L.M.S.R. 'Royal Scot' 4-6-0 engines introduced?
C In which year was the Forth Railway Bridge opened?
S What colour is the window sticker of the London–Bristol 'Brunel' service?
R The building that houses Swindon Railway Museum had what previous functions?
T At what pressure did the water tube boiler of L.N.E.R. 10000 work?
P What did Mrs. Jessie Scott-Batey inaugurate on 7 August 1980?

Q59
L For each b.h.p. how many pounds did each production 'Deltic' locomotive weigh?
C When did the G.W.R. close Bullo Pill Harbour, Gloucestershire, to coal traffic?
S In 1986, where did the 'Pembroke Coast Holiday Express' run from London?
R Which railway began operating on 15 September 1830?
T Which B.R. coach sub-mark introduced tinted non-opening windows in 1970?
P Who was Chairman of the British Transport Commission in 1953?

Q60 **L** David Shepherd aboard 92203. *(A.M. Drewett)*

A57 **L** 1967.
    C The London and North Western Railway.
    S The Great Western Railway.
    R 1968.
    T Swindon Works.
    P David Gentleman.

A58 **L** 1927.
    C 1890.
    S Yellow.
    R A Wesleyan Chapel, and before that a lodging house.
    T 450 pounds per square inch.
    P The Tyne and Wear Metro.

A59 **L** 67.
    C 1926.
    S Pembroke Dock.
    R The Liverpool and Manchester Railway.
    T Mark 2d.
    P Sir Brian Robertson.

Q60
- **L** What has railway artist David Shepherd named his '9F' 92203?
- **C** In which county was the 1 in 14 gradient of the Cromford and High Peak Railway located?
- **S** From which London terminus did the former 'Bournemouth Belle' run?
- **R** When did the East and West coast railways first 'race' to Scotland?
- **T** What colour is the chevron on the yellow face of a 'distant' semaphore signal?
- **P** Who wrote 'Thomas the Tank Engine'?

Q61
- **L** Which livery was 'Baby Deltic' D5909 unique in carrying within its class?
- **C** In which year was the current Tay Bridge opened?
- **S** Where does the 'Merchant Venturer' service run from London?
- **R** Which one of the 'Big Four' operated Barnwood engine shed, Gloucester?
- **T** What function do Class 930 departmental electric unit vehicles perform?
- **P** The final four C.M.E.s of the G.W.R. all served in what other capacity?

Q62
- **L** In which year was pioneer main-line diesel 10000 withdrawn?
- **C** The causeway between Portmadoc and Boston Lodge on the Ffestiniog line is called what?
- **S** Where was the signal box at Bath G.W.R. Station unusually situated?
- **R** Which regional P.T.E. had a broad green stripe on grey as its livery?
- **T** In four aspect signalling, which display immediately precedes green?
- **P** What did Mr. Keith Grand unveil at Swindon on 18 March 1960?

Q63
- **L** What livery did D5500 wear whilst 'running in' during October 1957?
- **C** Which Scottish bridge was designed by Sir Benjamin Baker and Sir John Fowler?
- **S** To which city does 'The Red Dragon' express run from London?
- **R** How many shades of blue feature in B.R.'s 'Trans Pennine' livery?
- **T** On what voltage does B.R.'s Waterloo and City line operate?
- **P** Who presented the B.B.C. television series 'Steam Days'?

Q64
- **L** What did Brush Electrical Engineering name diesel 10800 in 1962?
- **C** The Brecon Mountain and Ravenglass and Eskdale Railways are both built on what?
- **S** To which station does 'The Golden Hind' service run from London?
- **R** The pre-production A.P.T. bore the arms of which city?
- **T** What headlamp code denotes an express passenger train?
- **P** In 1985, who was President of the Guild of Railway Artists?

A60 **L** 'Black Prince'.
  C Derbyshire.
  S Waterloo.
  R 1888.
  T Black.
  P The Reverend Wilbert Awdry.

A61 **L** B.R. blue.
  C 1887.
  S Bristol.
  R The London, Midland and Scottish Railway.
  T De-icing of conductor rails.
  P Justice of the Peace.

A62 **L** 1963.
  C The Cob.
  S Over the roof of the down platform.
  R West Yorkshire Passenger Transport Executive.
  T Double amber.
  P The nameplate and plaque on 92220 'Evening Star'.

A63 **L** Brown, with a white band.
  C The Forth Bridge.
  S Swansea.
  R Two.
  T 660 volts d.c.
  P Miles Kington.

A64 **L** 'Hawk'.
  C The trackbeds of preceding railways.
  S Penzance.
  R The City of Derby.
  T Two lamps on either end of the locomotive buffer beam.
  P The Hon. William McAlpine F.C.I.T.

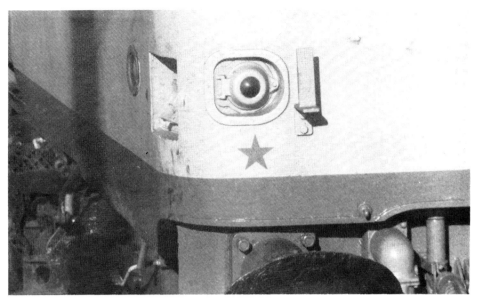

Q66 **R** A Class 37 Co-Co in the 'redstripe' livery variant. *(A.M. Drewett)*

Q65 **L** Which exhibit arrived at the Science Museum on 28 April 1963?
C Who designed the Royal Border Bridge at Berwick-on-Tweed?
S Which station has Britain's second longest platform?
R In which year did the G.W.R. introduce its first diesel railcar?
T B.R. Class 504 E.M.U.s run on what voltage from the conductor rails?
P Which railway trade union was founded by Charles Perry?

Q66 **L** When new, where were the first twenty Class 20 diesels allocated?
C When was the last demolition work completed on the Severn Railway Bridge?
S At which end of Swindon Station is Platform 2, the D.M.U. bay?
R Which sector has a livery variant known as 'redstripe'?
T Travellers Fare uses whose coffee in its 'Max Pax' system?
P Which railway pioneer was born at Wylam-on-Tyne in 1781?

Q67 **L** In which month and year were the last three Class 44 diesels withdrawn?
C How did George Stephenson take the L. and M.R. over Chat Moss?
S Before 1939, what was 'The Cornish Riviera Express' also known as?
R Which preserved railway links Pickering with Grosmont?
T What control system is fitted to Class 83 electric engines?
P Who designed the 1829 Rainhill Trials contender 'Sanspareil'?

A65 **L** The prototype 'Deltic'.
       C Robert Stephenson.
       S Colchester.
       R 1934.
       T 1200 volts d.c.
       P The Amalgamated Society of Locomotive Engineers and Firemen.

A66 **L** Devons Road Shed, East London.
       C 1970.
       S The Western end.
       R Railfreight.
       T Maxwell House.
       P George Stephenson.

A67 **L** November 1980.
       C The Line was 'floated' across on a brushwood raft.
       S 'The 10.30 Limited'.
       R The North Yorkshire Moors Railway.
       T Low tension tap changing.
       P Timothy Hackworth.

Q71 **R** Spot the Network South East colours. *(A.M. Drewett)*

Q68 **L** Whose engines powered the twenty pilot scheme Class 31 diesels?
       C How high is the loading gauge on Irish main 5'3" gauge lines?
       S In 1986, where did the 'Torbay Express' run from London?
       R How many Class 47 diesels were painted Brunswick Green in 1985?
       T What two voltages are Class 302 E.M.U.s designed to work on?
       P Who owns the Bressingham Gardens Railway, Norfolk?

Q69 **L** In which part of a Class 20 diesel are the air horns located?
       C When was the line from Wootton Bassett to Patchway via Badminton opened?
       S Which town is served by Pen Mill Station?
       R Which two cities' armorial bearings are incorporated in the G.W.R. crest?
       T What indication does a horizontal 'stop' semaphore signal give to trains?
       P Which historian completed E.T. MacDermot's three volume G.W.R. history?

Q70 **L** What name links 'Peak' 45144 and H.S.T. power car 43194?
       C Who designed the High Level Bridge over the Tyne at Newcastle?
       S Which named express linked Paddington and Aberystwyth in the 1950s?
       R In which year did B.R. abolish third class train accommodation?
       T What two voltages are Class 319 E.M.U.s designed to work on?
       P Which railway was founded by Captain J.E.P. Howey in 1925?

Q71 **L** When were Vale of Rheidol engines 7 'Owain Glyndwr' and 8 'Llwelyn' introduced?
       C Which bridge has the legend 'I.K. BRUNEL ENGINEER 1859' inscribed upon it?
       S The G.W.R. served two stations named Bampton. In which two counties were they?
       R From left to right, what three colours make the N.S.E. logo?
       T On which side of his cab did the driver of a G.W.R. steam engine sit?
       P Which animal appears in all the railway paintings of Terence Cuneo?

Q72 **L** B.R. Class 56 and 58 diesels share which coupling code?
       C In which county is Box Tunnel located?
       S Which is the southernmost terminus of the Dart Valley Railway?
       R When did B.R. take over the operation of British Pullman Coaches?
       T The 'People Mover' at Birmingham International station works on what principle?
       P J.H. Thomas M.P. was General Secretary of which trade union 1916–1931?

A68 **L** Mirrlees.
    C 13 feet 3 inches.
    S Paignton.
    R Four.
    T 25000 volts a.c. and 6250 volts a.c.
    P Alan Bloom.

A69 **L** In the roof, at the front of the cab.
    C 1903.
    S Yeovil.
    R London and Bristol.
    T Danger.
    P C.R. Clinker.

A70 **L** 'Royal Signals'.
    C Robert Stephenson.
    S 'The Cambrian Coast Express'.
    R 1956.
    T 25000 volts a.c. and 750 volts d.c.
    P The Romney, Hythe and Dymchurch Railway.

A71 **L** 1923.
    C The Royal Albert Bridge, Saltash.
    S Devon and Oxfordshire.
    R Red, blue and grey.
    T The right.
    P A mouse.

A72 **L** Red Diamond.
    C Wiltshire.
    S Kingswear.
    R 1955.
    T Magnetic Levitation.
    P The National Union of Railwaymen.

Q74 **S** D856 'Trojan' waits at Swindon. August 1962. *(W.G. Drewett)*

Q73 **L** Which preserved N.B.R. engine was withdrawn as B.R. 62469?
C Which river is spanned by Maidenhead Bridge, Berkshire?
S To which county did 'The Royal Duchy' express run?
R Why were the numbers of G.W.R. engines uniquely unchanged in 1948?
T At night, what colour light does a distant semaphore signal at caution display?
P Who described the G.W.R. as 'the finest work in England'?

Q74 **L** The 'U.S.A.' 0-6-0T locomotives were sold to the S.R. by whom?
C Digswell Viaduct is located 21½ miles north of which London terminus?
S When did 'Warship' diesel-hydraulics replace steam on the 'Bristolian' service?
R When did the Government cease controlling British railways after World War One?
T B.R. Class 89 engines have what type of control system?
P Braithwaite and Ericsson put in what for the Rainhill Trials?

Q75 **L** What are B.R. Class 91 electric engines known as?
C Which bridge has the longest cast iron spans ever built?
S What purpose does the old Fairford station, Gloucestershire, now serve?
R Prior to 1923, which two companies operated the 'west coast' route to Scotland?
T When did B.R. locomotives cease displaying train headcodes?
P What revolutionary invention did Thomas Edmondson make in 1836?

Q77 **R** 37710 in Railfreight Metals markings at Gloucester. *(A.M. Drewett)*

A73 **L** 'Glen Douglas' (N.B.R. 256).
     C River Thames.
     S Cornwall.
     R They had cast number plates, other lines used painted numbers.
     T Either yellow or orange.
     P Isambard Kingdom Brunel.

A74 **L** The U.S. Army Corps of Transportation.
     C Kings Cross.
     S June 1959.
     R August 1921.
     T Thyristor.
     P 'Novelty'.

A75 **L** 'Electras'.
     C The High Level Bridge, Newcastle-upon-Tyne.
     S It is now a coal yard.
     R The London and North Western and Caledonian Railways.
     T January 1976.
     P The first card railway ticket.

Q76
L G.W.R. engine 4900 'Saint Martin' was the prototype of which class?
C How wide are each of the arches of Brunel's Maidenhead Bridge?
S Which Welsh name has been given to Barmouth Junction?
R In 1939, how many private owner wagons operated on the 'Big Four' railways?
T A circular red and white signal relaying displays from a 'stop' signal is called what?
P S.Y. Griffith was the first lessee of which railway establishment?

Q77
L Where did Southern Railway '02' engines W14−W36 last work?
C When was the King Edward Bridge opened over the River Tyne?
S From what material were the 'pagoda' station shelters of the G.W.R. made?
R Which Railfreight sub-sector handles the movement of fly-ash?
T How many positions had the disc code train reporting system of the S.R.?
P Edward Pease, financier of the Stockton and Darlington, was a what?

Q78
L Who built the first 'Black Five' to enter service in 1934?
C In which year was the original Tay Bridge opened?
S Where does the Henley-on-Thames branch join the W.R. main line?
R Where is the Operations Centre of the Docklands Light Railway sited?
T What colour is the stripe on the white face of a semaphore signal?
P Until 1953, who was Chief Mechanical Engineer of B.R.?

Q79
L Parts from 6399 'Fury' were built into which 'Royal Scot' 4-6-0?
C Which bridge has its central tower on the Isle of Inchgarvie?
S Which station in Derbyshire opened on 5 July 1987?
R Which L.R.T. line is shown in green on the Tube map?
T From 1970 to 1976, Freightliner headcodes had which first digit?
P Lord Cawdor resigned as G.W.R. Chairman to become what?

Q80
L In which B.R. works were the S.R. Class 71 electric engines built?
C The three tunnels between Hadley Wood and Potters Bar have what internal diameter?
S In the 1960s, 'The Condor' express freight service linked which two cities?
R The armorial bearings of the M.R. and G.W.R. share which cities' crest?
T In a 4-digit headcode, what do 'x' and 'z' in the second column denote?
P Who organised his first tour to Loughborough in 1840?

A76 **L** 'Hall'.
      C 128 feet.
      S Morfa Mawddach.
      R 584000.
      T A banner signal.
      P Swindon station refreshment room.

A77 **L** The Isle of Wight.
      C 1906.
      S Corrugated iron.
      R Railfreight Construction.
      T Six.
      P Quaker.

A78 **L** The Vulcan Foundry.
      C 1878.
      S Twyford.
      R Poplar.
      T Black.
      P Robert A. Riddles C.B.E.

A79 **L** 46170 'British Legion'.
      C The Forth Bridge.
      S Chee Dale Halt.
      R The District Line.
      T '4'.
      P The First Lord of the Admiralty.

A80 **L** Doncaster.
      C 26 feet 6 inches.
      S London and Glasgow.
      R Bristol.
      T Special workings or excursion trains.
      P Thomas Cook.

Q81 **L** A Mark 2 T.S.O. data panel. *(A.M. Drewett)*

Q81 **L** In coaching stock, what do the letters T.S.O. stand for?
C The Britannia and Conway Bridges were designed by Robert Stephenson for whom?
S What are the two current stations at Windsor and Eton called?
R Which English railway painted its locomotives 'Improved Engine Green'?
T What indication does a vertical 'Somersalt' signal give?
P Who starred in the 1937 film 'Oh! Mr Porter!'?

Q82 **L** Which unorthodox engine class did the S.R. introduce in March 1942?
C Between which two L.R.T. stations is Britain's longest tunnel located?
S The G.W.R. war memorial is on which platform at Paddington?
R Which Railfreight depot uses the symbol of a white rose?
T What type of signal sometimes has a black and white striped post?
P Stanley Holloway and Sid James appeared in which 1952 film?

Q83 **L** Where was 'celebrity' diesel 47305 allocated in 1987?
C Which river is spanned by Hawarden Bridge, Clwyd?
S How many stations serve Reading, Berkshire?
R Second class seats in Mk.3 'Executive' liveried stock are what colour?
T 'Dowmac' and 'Costain' appear frequently on which track item?
P Who opened the Dart Valley Railway on 21 May 1969?

A81   **L**   Tourist Second Open.
           C   The London and North Western Railway.
           S   Central and Riverside.
           R   The London, Brighton and South Coast Railway.
           T   Line clear ahead.
           P   Will Hay.

A82   **L**   Class 'Q-1'.
           C   East Finchley and Morden.
           S   Platform One.
           R   Tinsley, Sheffield.
           T   A distant signal.
           P   'The Titfield Thunderbolt'.

A83   **L**   Thornaby.
           C   River Dee.
           S   Two.
           R   Red.
           T   Concrete sleepers.
           P   Lord Beeching.

Q87 T
What track
layout lies
ahead?
*(A.M.
Drewett)*

Q84
L What was the last Birmingham R.C.W. locomotive named?
C A rolling lifting bridge carries the Doncaster–Grimsby line over what at Keadby?
S How was the 'Cheltenham Flyer' described in G.W. timetables before 1939?
R When was the Brecon and Merthyr Railway absorbed by the G.W.R.?
T On the L.N.W.R., what did ringed signal arms control?
P What was George Hudson of York popularly known as?

Q85
L 46100 'Royal Scot' was displayed at which Butlin's camp in the '60s?
C In which county is Chipping Sodbury Tunnel, W.R., located?
S How do passengers cross the lines at Bristol Parkway station?
R Four black diamonds on yellow is the symbol of which Railfreight subsector?
T What in-cab signal means 'Line clear ahead' in a.w.s.?
P Which 'Railway Station' did William Powell Frith paint in 1862?

Q86
L Which 'A4' pacific was named after an American President?
C On average, how deep are the tunnels of the London Underground?
S The three slip portions of the 'Cornish Riviera Express' went where?
R 1957, how many miles of track did B.R. own and operate?
T What headlamp indication was used for a breakdown train not on duty?
P Where did Driver John Axon earn his George Cross in 1957?

Q87
L How many B.R. Standard steam classes were built?
C How many gallons of water are pumped out of the Severn Tunnel on average each day?
S Which city has stations named Shrub Hill and Foregate Street?
R Which railway links Toddington and Winchcombe, Gloucestershire?
T A row of white lights leaning to the left over a signal indicates what?
P In which year was E. Nesbitts book 'The Railway Children' published?

Q88
L When were 'Princess Royal' locomotives 6200 and 6201 built?
C When was the third Woodhead Tunnel opened?
S When did Savernake and Wootton Rivers Stations, Wiltshire close?
R What was the B.R. stock emblem used from 1956 to 1966 known as?
T What equipment is controlled by the black levers in a manual signal box?
P Philip Hardwick designed what part of the original Euston Station?

A84 **L** D0260 'Lion'.
        C The Trent Navigation.
        S 'Cheltenham Spa Express–Tea Car Train'.
        R July 1922.
        T 'Slow' lines.
        P 'The Railway King'.

A85 **L** Skegness.
        C Avon.
        S By means of a footbridge.
        R Railfreight Coal.
        T A bell rings.
        P London Paddington.

A86 **L** 60008 'Dwight D. Eisenhower'.
        C 90 feet.
        S Weymouth, Ilfracombe and Minehead.
        R 18965 miles.
        T One lamp, on the top central bracket.
        P Chapel-en-le-Frith, Derbyshire.

A87 **L** Twelve.
        C 20 million gallons.
        S Worcester.
        R The Gloucestershire and Warwickshire Railway.
        T A track diverges from the main line, ahead to the left.
        P 1906.

A88 **L** 1933.
        C 1954.
        S 1966.
        R 'The Ferret and Dartboard'.
        T Points.
        P The Doric Portico.

Q90 L 73129 'City of Winchester'. *(A.M. Drewett)*

Q89 L Apart from 4771, where did 'V2' engines carry their nameplates?
C What do 'C' and 'T' signs tell train drivers about engineering work?
S At Paddington, what is the soldier in the war memorial sculpture doing?
R Which railway museum opened on 27 September 1975?
T A signal that lets a train past a danger signal into an occupied block is called what?
P Which work of composer Vivian Ellis was inspired by an L.M.S. train?

Q90 L S.R. Class 73 electro-diesels have which make of engine?
C On which region was the first mile-plus length of C.W.R. track laid?
S How many passengers travelled on the last train out of Devizes in 1966?
R Where were the locomotive works of the L. and N.W.R. located?
T In 1957, what was the standard length of point-protecting locking bar on B.R.?
P On 1 August 1850, Queen Victoria opened what?

Q91 L Where were the first forty L.N.E.R. 'B1' 4-6-0s built?
C How far apart are wooden sleepers spaced in British practice?
S In 1986, where was Britain's best kept station located?
R Which two animals held up the Midland Railway coat of arms?
T In a W.R. 4-digit headcode, what destination does a letter 'C' indicate?
P What did Charles Tayleur found at Newton-le-Willows in 1830?

Q92 **L** A thirsty job for 56053 as 87101 fails to sap the juice. *(John Chalcraft)*

A89 **L** Over the centre pair of driving wheels.
  C Where the work Commences and Terminates.
  S Reading a letter.
  R The National Railway Museum, York.
  T A 'calling on' signal.
  P 'Coronation Scot'.

A90 **L** English Electric.
  C Southern Region.
  S Fifteen.
  R Crewe.
  T 40 feet.
  P The Royal Border Bridge, Berwick on Tweed.

A91 **L** Darlington.
  C 2 feet 6 inches.
  S Dumfries, Strathclyde.
  R A fish and a chameleon.
  T Cardiff.
  P The Vulcan Foundry.

Q92
L What is the fuel capacity of a B.R. Class 56 diesel?
C Which junction was first to be remodelled with a flyover for the L.M.R. electrification?
S Where did the Weymouth slip portion leave the down '10.30 Limited'?
R Which railway published the tourist guide 'Holiday Haunts' before 1939?
T In a manual signal box, what colour are unused levers painted?
P The Moorish Arch at Edge Hill, Liverpool, was built for whom?

Q93
L Which Swindon-built 'Warship' had a name unconnected with the Royal Navy?
C What was the World's first cable-stayed railway suspension bridge built to span?
S To which two ports did 'The Golden Arrow' run from London?
R Which railway began operations on 31 August 1987?
T The track-mounted tread plates that monitor vehicle presence are called what?
P Who wrote the poem about T.P.O.s called 'The Night Mail'?

Q94
L Which diesel class replaced Southampton Docks 'U.S.A.' 0-6-0 Ts?
C On what part of the permanent way are stretcher-bars found?
S In 1980, the fastest Stevenage–Peterborough passenger service averaged what?
R Which railway is financially supported by Redland Roof Tiles Ltd?
T Who makes the door window fittings of B.R. Mk.2 coaches?
P Who was Chairman of the British Transport Commission in 1948?

Q95
L Which Bo-Bo diesel electric of 1962 had two Paxman engines?
C How many bridges had to be raised for the L.M.R. electrification to Liverpool and Manchester?
S Which is British Rail's highest station?
R The arms of the Ffestiniog Railway contains which Royal emblem?
T What does the letter 'V' denote in a 4-digit headcode?
P Sir Eustace Missenden was the last General Manager of what?

Q96
L Who built 0-4-0 departmental diesel DS1169 in 1946?
C Up to 1956 Whitemoor, Toton and Hull were the location of Britain's principle what?
S Which engine hauled the 'Royal Sunset' rail tour on 26 September 1987?
R Which depot applies the symbol of a lizard to its engines?
T What do the blue levers in a manual signal box control?
P When did Sir William Stanier resign as C.M.E. of the L.M.S.?

A92 **L** 1150 gallons.
        C Bletchley.
        S Westbury.
        R The Great Western Railway.
        T White.
        P The Liverpool and Manchester Railway.

A93 **L** D800 'Sir Brian Robertson'.
        C The M25 motorway.
        S Folkestone and Dover.
        R The Docklands Light Railway.
        T Fouling bars.
        P Whystan Hugh Auden.

A94 **L** Class 07.
        C Points.
        S 106.25 m.p.h.
        R The Leighton Buzzard Narrow Gauge Railway.
        T Beclawatt Ltd.
        P Sir Cyril Hurcomb.

A95 **L** 'Clayton' Class 17.
        C 904.
        S Corrour, Inverness-shire.
        R The Prince of Wales feathers.
        T Western Region.
        P The Southern Railway.

A96 **L** The Bristol Aeroplane Company.
        C Mechanised marshalling yards.
        S 6000 'King George V'.
        R Par St. Blazey, Cornwall.
        T Locking bars.
        P 1944.

Q97 C Runaway trains stop here! *(A.M. Drewett)*

Q97 L B.R. locomotives with electro-pneumatic control have which coupling code?
C What are the p.w. devices used to derail runaway vehicles called?
S When was the station at Ilfracombe, Devon, closed?
R The bearings of which railway showed a lion surmounted by a castle?
T Until May 1969, what did a single lamp on the left of a locomotive buffer beam denote?
P Who was Robert Riddle's first Executive Officer, Design, on B.R.?

Q98 L 'Kidwelly' and 'Ashburnham' are names from which B.R. sub-class?
C What is the name of the freight yard at Margam begun in November 1987?
S Before 1939, what was the first stop of the down 'Cornish Riviera Express?
R Which railway was the first to offer road motor bus services?
T What does a bell ringing four times in even succession mean to a signalman?
P Who did C.E. Fairburn leave to join the L.M.S.?

Q99 L What is the sole member of B.R. electric Class 87/1 named?
C How much of the Severn Tunnel is actually under the Severn?
S In 1980, Britain's heaviest goods train ran from Port Talbot to where?
R Which railway operates over part of the ex-L.S.W.R. Seaton branch?
T When did the L.M.S. fit its first magneto-inductive a.t.c. system?
P S.B. Warder won a gold medal for his part in what?

A97 **L** Blue star.
 C Catch points.
 S October 1970.
 R The North Staffordshire Railway.
 T Light engine.
 P E.S. Cox.

A98 **L** Class 08/9.
 C Knuckle Yard.
 S Plymouth.
 R The Great Western Railway.
 T 'Is the line clear for an express train?'.
 P English Electric.

A99 **L** 'Stephenson'.
 C 2¼ miles.
 S Llanwern steelworks, South Wales.
 R The Seaton and District Electric Tramway.
 T 1938.
 P Electrifying the line from Euston to Liverpool.

Q102 S Not so blue a Pullman passes Twyford. *(Diesel Traction Group)*

Q100 **L** What are W.R. Class 142 railbuses known as?
　　　C How many feet above sea level is the summit of the Snaefell Mountain Railway?
　　　S Which British Rail Station has the most platforms?
　　　R What is Rheilfford Llyn Tegid known as in English?
　　　T All four headcode lamp brackets are only used on what type of train?
　　　P Who directed the film 'Return to Waterloo'?

Q101 **L** In December 1986, 'Tamworth Castle' was the only 'namer' of which B.R. class?
　　　C Where would an array of 'King', 'Queen' and 'Jack' points be found?
　　　S Until 1939, what shaped head board had the 'Cheltenham Spa Express'?
　　　R Which ficticious railway appeared in the film 'The Railway Children'?
　　　T What does the acronym B.R.U.T.E. stand for?
　　　P Which Army Corps did H.G. Ivatt serve in during the Great War?

Q102 **L** How many B.R. diesels have been named after British Royalty?
　　　C Which river was spanned, near Buildwas, by the Albert Edward Bridge?
　　　S Which company built the W.R. 'Blue Pullman' trains of the 1960s?
　　　R Which company's logo appears on Waterloo and City line trains?
　　　T When was panel-operated route setting fitted at Thirsk by the L.N.E.R.?
　　　P Sidney Newey directs which B.R. sector?

Q103 **L** How many 'Deltic' locomotives were named after racehorses?
　　　C How many feet above sea level is Ais Gill summit?
　　　S In 1980, which was Britain's busiest junction station?
　　　R On which of the British Isles is the Snaefell Mountain Railway sited?
　　　T What is the frequency of a.c. used in the L.M.R. electrification?
　　　P Author Robert Adley is an M.P. for which political party?

Q104 **L** How many Class 47 diesels have been named after George Cross holders?
　　　C Where did the L.N.W.R. build its first gravity marshalling yard?
　　　S Where did the 'Queen of Scots' Pullman run from London?
　　　R Two red diamonds on yellow symbolise which Railfreight sub-sector?
　　　T The London–Southend catenary was electrified to what voltage in 1950?
　　　P Eric Treacy was the Bishop of where?

A100 **L** 'Skippers'.
        C 2034 feet.
        S Waterloo.
        R The Bala Lake Railway.
        T A Royal train.
        P Ray Davies (also lead singer of 'The Kinks').

A101 **L** Class 25.
        C In a hump marshalling yard.
        S Rectangular.
        R The Great Northern and Southern.
        T British Rail Universal Trolley Equipment.
        P The Royal Army Service Corps.

A102 **L** Two-33027 'Earl Mountbatten of Burma' and 47541 'The Queen Mother'.
        C River Severn.
        S Metropolitan Cammell.
        R Allied Lyons.
        T 1933.
        P Provincial Services.

A103 **L** Eight.
        C 1167 feet.
        S Clapham Junction, Southern Region.
        R The Isle of Man.
        T 50 Hertz.
        P The Conservative Party.

A104 **L** Three.
        C Edge Hill, Liverpool.
        S Edinburgh.
        R Speedlink Distribution.
        T 1500 volts d.c.
        P Wakefield, West Yorkshire.

Q105 L 50018 'Resolution' pauses at Bristol Temple Meads. *(Steve Turner).*

Q105 L How many English Electric Class 50 diesels have been built?
C When was the last of Brunel's Cornish timber viaducts replaced?
S On 10 April 1979 an H.S.T. speed record was set between London and where?
R Which is Britain's most northerly preserved railway?
T What do the yellow levers in a mechanical signal box operate?
P Which Gloucestershire town was home to Sir Felix Pole of the G.W.R.?

Q106 L B.R. engine 86234 is named after which old Mancunian?
C When were Charing Cross and Blackfriars railway bridges built?
S From which London terminus did the 'Brighton Belle' service run?
R Complete the slogan 'I always go south for sunshine by . . .'
T Which of the 'Big Four' used corridor tenders for non-stop runs?
P Which C.M.E. of the L.N.E.R. died in April 1941?

Q107 L What does the acronym T.R.U.B. stand for?
C Brunel's Chepstow Wye Bridge was the model for which later structure?
S In which year was the current Euston Station opened?
R When did the Canterbury and Whitstable Railway open?
T In 1958, what was B.R.'s maximum speed for short 2-axle vehicles?
P In 1980, Karen Harrison became W.R.'s first what?

Q109 **L** Class 15 Bo-Bo D8209 at Devons Road on 5 April 1959. *(Authors Collection)*

A105 **L** Fifty.
     C 1934.
     S Chippenham, Wiltshire.
     R The Strathspey Railway.
     T Distant signals.
     P Stroud.

A106 **L** J.B. Priestley.
     C 1864.
     S Victoria.
     R '. . . Southern'.
     T The London and North Eastern Railway.
     P Sir Nigel Gresley.

A107 **L** Trailer Restaurant Unclassified Buffet.
     C The Royal Albert Bridge, Saltash.
     S 1968.
     R 1830.
     T 60 m.p.h.
     P Female trainee train driver.

Q108 **L** How many Class 52 'Western diesels have been preserved?
       C Of what material was the Adam Viaduct, Wigan, built in 1947?
       S To which city did the L.N.E.R. 'Silver Jubilee' service run from London?
       R Which is Britain's longest preserved railway?
       T Why did the L.N.E.R. fit rubber sheets between the coaches of its streamlined trains?
       P Who starred in the 1931 film 'The Ghost Train'?

Q109 **L** Where is the sole example of B.R. diesel Class 15 preserved?
       C Which river is spanned by Landore Viaduct, between Swansea and Neath?
       S Which S.R. Pullman express first ran on 20 June 1947?
       R When did B.R. begin its Dover–Bologne hovercraft service?
       T Red and white lamps encircled by matching discs indicate what type of train?
       P What did G.W.R. engineer C. Richardson do for cricket players?

Q110 **L** What do the initials T.L.U.K. stand for?
       C What links Connel Ferry Bridge, Strathclyde and Tower Bridge?
       S In 1877, where was the World's largest railway station located?
       R Which railway links Oxenhope with Keighley?
       T When was the last British Rail T.P.O. lineside pick up made?
       P Which private in Dad's Army wrote 'The Ghost Train'?

Q111 **L** Class 9714 departmental vehicles share which wheel arrangement?
       C Some of the ironwork in the Royal Albert Bridge was originally designed for what?
       S In Spring 1927, the down 'Royal Scot' made its first stop where?
       R When did the Mid-Suffolk Light Railway join the L.N.E.R.?
       T In what type of bridge would masonry 'jack arches' be found?
       P In which year did Sir Sam Fay, late of the G.C.R. die?

Q112 **L** When did the first B.R. standard coach designs enter service?
       C When were the tubes of the Britannia Bridge wrecked by fire?
       S Before 1952, what was the E.C.M.L. 'Elizabethan' service called?
       R On which railways service would a Train Captain be found?
       T What are Greathead Shields and Price Rotary Excavators used for?
       P When did Bishop Eric Treacy sadly die?

A108 **L** Seven.
        C Pre-stressed concrete.
        S Newcastle-upon-Tyne.
        R The West Somerset Railway.
        T To reduce air resistance.
        P Jack Hulbert and Cicely Courtneidge.

A109 **L** Bury Transport Museum.
        C River Tawe.
        S 'The Devon Belle'.
        R 1968.
        T A slip portion from a non-stop express train.
        P He made the first bat with a spliced cane handle.

A110 **L** Trailer Lounge Unclassified Kitchen.
        C Both were designed by Sir John Wolfe Barry.
        S York.
        R The Keighley and Worth Valley Railway.
        T 1971.
        P Private Godfrey (alias Arnold Ridley).

A111 **L** 1 Co-Col.
        C Clifton Suspension Bridge, Bristol.
        S Carnforth, Lancashire.
        R July 1924.
        T A girder bridge.
        P 1953.

A112 **L** 1951.
        C 1970.
        S 'The Capitals Limited'.
        R The Docklands Light Railway.
        T Tunneling.
        P May 1978.

Q113 L B.R. Mark 2 stock at London Paddington on 10 July 1988. *(A.M. Drewett)*

Q113 L When was the prototype Mk.2 coach introduced by B.R.?
      C Which is the tallest viaduct on the Settle–Carlisle Railway?
      S Which was the last major London terminus to be built?
      R What do the initials A.S.L.E.F. stand for?
      T The red levers in a mechanical signal box control what?
      P C.M. Cock was the last Chief Electrical Engineer of which railway?

Q114 L Coaches named 'Lowri' and 'Myfanwy' ran on which part of B.R.?
      C Apart from a railway, what did Luxulyan Viaduct, Cornwall, carry?
      S Which London terminus has plaques reading 'THE BUTTERLEY COMPANY, DERBYSHIRE'?
      R Who said of Cornwall 'See your own Country first'?
      T Which British railway uses the Abt system of rack adhesion?
      P What made Thomas Walker say 'One subaqueous tunnel is enough'?

Q115 L Which S.R. class 'V' engine is preserved in the U.S.A.?
      C Which river is spanned by Ballochmyle Viaduct, Scotland?
      S Which Birmingham suburb is served by Rolfe Street station?
      R Who flew a flag from Porth Penrhyn Station when its trains ran?
      T Whose 'Pacific' engines were built with a chain driven motion?
      P Who answered questions on British Steam Locomotives to be 'Mastermind'?

A113 L 1963.
  C Smardale Viaduct.
  S Marylebone.
  R Amalgamated Society of Locomotive Engineers and Firemen.
  T Stop signals.
  P The Southern Railway.

A114 L The Vale of Rheidol Railway.
  C An aqueduct.
  S St. Pancras.
  R The Great Western Railway.
  T The Snowdon Mountain Railway.
  P The Severn Tunnel.

A115 L 30926 'Repton'.
  C River Ayr.
  S Smethwick.
  R The Fairbourne Railway.
  T The Southern Railway.
  P Christopher Hughes.

A117 R The Nene Valleys Wansford Signal Box. *(A.M. Drewett)*

Q116 **L** How many wheels does Royal Train Sleeper Power Brake 2910 have?
      C For which railway was Wharncliffe Viaduct built in 1837?
      S When was the 'Morning Talisman' E.C.M.L. service introduced?
      R In which city is British Rails Railway Technical Centre located?
      T Which L.M.S. class had steam powered coal pushers fitted to its tenders?
      P Who opened the East Somerset Railway on 20 June 1975?

Q117 **L** When was Mark 2a coaching stock introduced by British Rail?
      C How many rivets are used to hold the Forth Bridge together?
      S On which Swindon Station platform is the Joint Services Air Trooping Centre?
      R In which county is the Nene Valley Railway located?
      T What was the maximum amount of tilt achieved by the A.P.T.?
      P L.M.R. diesel-mechanical locomotive 10100 was designed by whom?

Q118 **L** What were Great Western 'Mogo' wagons built to carry?
      C Welland Viaduct, Northamptonshire, is built of which two colours of brick?
      S The Railair Lounge is located on which Reading station platform?
      R According to its former slogan 'British Rail makes the going . . .' what?
      T The only L.M.S. Schmidt-boilered engine was introduced when?
      P Of which transport organisation was F. Pope Chairman in 1952?

Q119 **L** What type of wagon would have a 3-letter T.O.P.S. code starting with a 'J'?
      C Which river is spanned by Sankey Viaduct, Earlestown, Merseyside?
      S Which Scottish city once had a station named Princes Street?
      R What do the initials A.R.P.S. stand for?
      T Who re-signalled the St. Pancras–Sharnbrook route in the 1980s?
      P In 1947, H.G. Ivatt became a consultant to which company?

Q120 **L** Which L.M.S. 'Royal Scot' set a World non-stop distance record in April 1928?
      C Wharncliffe Viaduct, W.R. bears whose coat of arms on its south side?
      S When did both the 'up' and 'down' 'Talisman' depart each day in 1956?
      R In Executive-liveried H.S.T.s, what colour are the Trailer Second carpets?
      T Which Rainhill Trials engine of 1829 had a multi-tube boiler?
      P Whose autobiography is titled 'The Man who loves Giants'?

A116 **L** Twelve.
C The Great Western Railway.
S 1957.
R Derby.
T 'Princess Coronation'.
P Prince Bernhard of The Netherlands.

A117 **L** 1967.
C 6.5 million.
S Platform 3.
R Cambridgeshire.
T 9 degrees.
P Colonel L.F.R. Fell.

A118 **L** Motor cars.
C Red and blue.
S Platform 5.
R '. . . easy!'
T 1929.
P The Ulster Transport Authority.

A119 **L** A bogie coil wagon.
C Sankey Brook.
S Edinburgh.
R The Association of Railway Preservation Societies.
T Westinghouse Signals.
P Brush Electrical Engineering Ltd.

A120 **L** 46113 'Cameronian'.
C Lord Wharncliffes.
S 4 p.m.
R Grey.
T Stephensons 'Rocket'.
P David Shepherd, the railway artist.